Judgments

RESOURCES FOR BIBLICAL LIVING

Bitterness: The Root That Pollutes
Deception: Letting Go of Lying
Divorce: Before You Say "I Don't"
Fear: Breaking Its Grip
Judgments: Rash or Righteous
Manipulation: Knowing How to Respond
Self-Image: How to Overcome Inferiority Judgments

Judgments

Rash or Righteous

LOU PRIOLO

PUBLISHING
P.O. BOX 817 • PHILLIPSBURG • NEW JERSEY 08865-0817

Printed in the United States of America

Library of Congress Cataloging-in-Publication Data

Priolo, Lou.
 Judgments : rash or righteous / Lou Priolo.
    p. cm. — (Resources for biblical living)
 Includes bibliographical references.
 ISBN 978-1-59638-120-9 (pbk.)
 1. Judgment—Religious aspects—Christianity. 2. Judgment—Biblical teaching. I. Title.
 BV4597.54.P75 2009
 241—dc22

                          2009006258

WHAT IN THE WORLD is a rash judgment? No, it is definitely *not* the diagnosis made by a dermatologist. A rash judgment is jumping to hasty and unfounded negative conclusions about another's character without having sufficient biblical cause. Although making *rash* or *snap judgments* (superficial, nondiscriminating, and presumptuous) is something we all have done, some people are especially prone to making them—not only about others, but also about God and the circumstances he has sovereignly decreed would come into their lives. If you are one of those people, this booklet may provide just the practical help and hope for which you've been waiting.

At best, a rash judgment is a violation of 1 Corinthians 13:7 (not believing the best about others) and thus is an uncharitable attitude. At worst, it is a violation of the ninth commandment: "You shall not bear false witness against your neighbor" (Ex. 20:16).

The historic Heidelberg Catechism asks and answers the following question:

What is required in the ninth commandment?

That I bear false witness against no man; wrest no one's words; be no backbiter or slanderer; *do not judge, or join in condemning any man rashly or unheard*; but that I avoid all sorts of lies and deceit as the proper works of the Devil, unless I would bring down upon myself the heavy wrath of God; likewise, that in judicial and all other dealings, I love the truth, speak it uprightly, and confess it; and that as much as I am able, I *defend and promote the honor and reputation of my neighbor.* (emphasis added)[1]

1. G. I. Williamson, *The Heidelberg Catechism: A Study Guide* (Phillipsburg, NJ: P&R Publishing, 1993), 201.

Judging rashly often involves making judgments about someone according to appearance rather than according to biblical principles. Jesus said in John 7:24, "Do not judge according to appearance, but judge with righteous judgment." On this occasion, it seemed to some who judged "according to appearance" that Jesus had broken the Sabbath laws. But according to righteous judgment, he had not. I have taken the liberty to paraphrase J. C. Ryle's thoughts on this passage.

> Nothing is so common as to judge too favorably or too unfavorably from merely looking at the outward appearance of things. We are apt to form hasty opinions of others, either for good or evil, on very insufficient grounds. We pronounce some men to be good and others to be bad, some to be godly and others to be ungodly, without anything but appearance to aid our decision. We should do well to remember our blindness, and to keep in mind this text. The bad are not always so bad, nor the good so good as they appear. A potsherd may be covered over with gold and look bright outside. A nugget of gold may be covered with dirt and look like worthless rubbish. One man's work may look good at first, and yet turn out by and by to have been done from the basest motives. Another man's work may look very questionable at first, and yet at last may prove Christlike and truly godly. May the Lord deliver us from rashly "judging by appearances"![2]

Jesus tells you not to make superficial judgments. He expects you to get below the surface and apply the Scriptures correctly to each circumstance. As we'll see in a moment, if you can't see below the surface, perhaps you ought to suspend your judgment until you can. Maybe it's not your place to make a judgment at all.

As Christians, we must be careful to make judgments on proven facts, not on superficial appearances. That's what Jesus

2. J. C. Ryle, *Expository Thoughts on the Gospels: For Family and Private Use* (New York: Robert Carter and Brothers, 1878), 26 (author's paraphrase).

did. Speaking of Christ, Isaiah prophesied, "He will not judge by what His eyes see, nor make a decision by what His ears hear; but with righteousness He will judge the poor, and decide with fairness for the afflicted of the earth" (Isa. 11:3–4).

But doesn't the Bible forbid us to judge? Actually, it says,

> Do not judge so that you will not be judged. For in the way you judge, you will be judged; and by your standard of measure, it will be measured to you. Why do you look at the speck that is in your brother's eye, but do not notice the log that is in your own eye? Or how can you say to your brother, "Let me take the speck out of your eye," and behold, the log is in your own eye? You hypocrite, first take the log out of your own eye, and then you will see clearly to take the speck out of your brother's eye. (Matt. 7:1–5)

This is probably one of the most familiar but misunderstood and misapplied passages in the Bible. Many believe this verse forbids making judgments of *any* kind. But that is clearly not the case. Look at the very next verse. "Do not give what is holy to *dogs*, and do not throw your pearls before *swine*, or they will trample them under their feet, and turn and tear you to pieces" (Matt. 7:6).

It takes a fair amount of discrimination when ministering the Word of God. In order to obey this command, you must evaluate or *judge* others, *discriminating* between *professing Christians* and *unbelievers*. Why do such judgments have to be made about different kinds of people? Because the "natural man does not accept the things of the Spirit of God, for they are foolishness to him; and he cannot understand them, because they are spiritually appraised" (1 Cor. 2:14). To try to remove the speck (reprove and counsel from Scripture) from those who do not have the ability to appreciate God's Word could result in disaster.

Now let's jump down to Matthew 7:15.

> Beware of the *false prophets*, who come to you in *sheep's clothing*, but inwardly are ravenous wolves. *You will know them by*

their fruits. Grapes are not gathered from thorn bushes, nor figs from thistles, are they? So every good tree bears good fruit, but the bad tree bears bad fruit. A good tree cannot produce bad fruit, nor can a bad tree produce good fruit. Every tree that does not bear good fruit is cut down and thrown into the fire. So then, *you will know them by their fruits.* (Matt. 7:15–20)

Christians are supposed to be discerning enough to spot false shepherds (it was the *shepherds*, not the sheep, who wore the sheep's clothing) by examining their fruits. The fruit of a false prophet can be severe character flaws, or false doctrine, or the kind of converts that he makes. All of these require some form of judgment to be made.

Judging for the Christian is the rule, not the exception. Indeed, "He who is spiritual judges all things, yet he himself is *rightly* judged by no one" (1 Cor. 2:15 NKJV). Why do you suppose the Bible contains so many characterological type verses (verses about the different kinds of people we might meet) if God did not expect us to discriminate between[3] different types of persons? Here are a few of the many biblical categories of the kinds of people God may bring across your path:

Angry	Double-Minded	Fearful
Gluttonous	Pleasure-Loving	Self-Willed
Backbiting	Drunk	Foolish
Gossiping	Money-Loving	Scornful
Boastful	Falsely Prophetic	Fornicating
Lying	Sluggish	Swindling

You will need a certain amount of discernment (righteous judgment) to identify them.

3. Please note, I did not say "discriminate against."

Three Exceptions

I know of three exceptions to the rule of judging (three things that we as Christians are *not* supposed to judge). As far as I can judge (pun intended), pretty much everything else is fair game.

Don't judge things to be sin that are not (explicitly or implicitly) identified as sin according to the Bible.

> Do not speak against one another, brethren. He who speaks against a brother or judges his brother, speaks against the law and judges the law; but if you judge the law, you are not a doer of the law, but a judge of it. (James 4:11)

"*So what* if the Bible does not condemn it. Everybody knows that it's a sin to do it."

When you judge things to be sinful that are not *clearly* delineated as such (at least in principle) in the Scriptures, you wrongly judge not only your brother who did the misjudged deed, but also the Bible for not condemning the deed, and the author of the Bible who "apparently" forgot to include it in Holy Writ. Think of how grave a matter it is to make such a presumptuous accusation against God!

Don't judge those things that God has hidden from you (i.e., things about which you have insufficient knowledge to make a sound judgment).

First Corinthians 4:5 is a key verse for understanding our human limitations when it comes to making judgments: "Therefore do not go on passing judgment before the time, *but wait* until the Lord comes who will both bring to light the things hidden in the darkness and disclose the motives of *men's* hearts; and then each man's praise will come to him from God."

Sometimes we cannot see "the things hidden in the darkness"—we simply do not have enough information to make a judgment because we don't have all the essential facts. Moreover, because we are not in a position to acquire the information necessary, we have no biblical option but to suspend judgment. People in positions of authority, however, often do have the right and the resources to investigate information that may be hidden from others: "It is the glory of God to conceal a matter, But the glory of kings is to search out a matter" (Prov. 25:2).

At other times, we may find ourselves in positions of authority in which we are not only required to act as judge, but to collect information that others may not have the ability or authority to collect (cf. Deut. 13:14; 17:4; 19:18). But unless we have been given such authority by God, in the absence of evidence we may simply have to hold off making any kind of hard-and-fast judgment until the Lord provides it.

If you should find yourself in such an authoritative position, consider the solemn responsibility that God has given you to act as a judge (cf. 1 Cor. 6:1–6) who makes righteous judgments only after a thorough investigation.

> If you hear in one of your cities, which the LORD your God is giving you to live in, anyone saying that some worthless men have gone out from among you and have seduced the inhabitants of their city, saying, "Let us go and serve other gods" (whom you have not known), then *you shall investigate and search out and inquire thoroughly.* If it is true and the matter established that this abomination has been done among you, you shall surely strike the inhabitants of that city with the edge of the sword, utterly destroying it and all that is in it and its cattle with the edge of the sword. (Deut. 13:12–15)

Don't judge the thoughts and motives of another person.

God has not given us the ability to know what is on the heart of another person apart from what he chooses to disclose to us. While we may rightly judge his thoughts, words, attitudes, and actions (because they are apparent), we may not presume to do what only God can do: judge the heart of another (cf. 1 Sam. 16:7).[4]

> But to me it is a very small thing that I should be examined by you, or by any human court; in fact, I do not even examine myself. For I am conscious of nothing against myself, yet I am not by this acquitted; but the one who examines me is the Lord. Therefore do not go on passing judgment before the time, but wait until the Lord comes who will both bring to light the things hidden in the darkness and disclose the motives of men's hearts; and then each man's praise will come to him from God. (1 Cor. 4:3–5)

There are many other passages that speak to the legitimacy of judging all sorts of things. Here are some of them:

> I say this to your shame. Is it so, that there is not among you one wise man who will be able to *decide* between his brethren? (1 Cor. 6:5)

> Do not participate in the unfruitful deeds of darkness, but instead even *expose* them. (Eph. 5:11)

> Now I urge you, brethren, *keep your eye on* those who cause dissensions and hindrances contrary to the teaching which you learned, and turn away from them. (Rom. 16:17)

> Reject a factious man after a first and second warning, knowing that such a man is perverted and is sinning, being self-condemned. (Titus 3:10–11)

> But *examine everything* carefully; hold fast to that which is good. (1 Thess. 5:21)

4. Of course, we may often be able to ask another to judge his own heart and disclose to us his self-evaluation. For example, as a biblical counselor interested in helping people change not just externally, but in their hearts, it is often my job to ask about their motives.

If your brother sins [against you], go and show him his fault in private; if he listens to you, you have won your brother. But if he does not listen to you, take one or two more with you, so that by the mouth of two or three witnesses every fact may be confirmed. If he refuses to listen to them, tell it to the church; and if he refuses to listen even to the church, let him be to you as a Gentile and a tax collector. (Matt. 18:15–17)

The point of listing these passages is simply to underscore the fact that judging *is the rule* for the Christian as long as it is done biblically. This booklet is intended to help you learn how to avoid making the *wrong* kinds of judgments.

Different Forms of Rash Judgments

The first step in avoiding these rash judgments is to recognize them for what they are. Here are some of the most common.

Attributing evil motives to someone

As I have explained, 1 Corinthians 4:5 forbids us to judge the intentions of others. Only God can rightly judge the hearts of men: "God *sees* not as man sees, for man looks at the outward appearance, but the LORD looks at the heart" (1 Sam. 16:7; cf. 1 Kings 8:39; 1 Chron. 28:9; Luke 16:15). Indeed, love requires us to believe the best about others (cf. 1 Cor. 13:7). More about this later.

Here are a few examples of motive judgments that I have come across in my years of counseling:

"You only said that because you want me to feel guilty."

"The reason you're being nice to me is so that I'll give you what you want."

"You only married me for my money (or good looks)."

"My mother doesn't want me to have fun."

"She wore that dress to show off her curves."

"She did that just to spite me!"

Unless the individuals in question have clearly stated their motives, we simply don't have the right (or ability) to presume to know them.

Judging based on insufficient evidence rather than facts

The same passage that tells us not to attribute evil motives to others (1 Cor. 4:5) also requires us to postpone judgment on things about which we don't have sufficient evidence.

The danger and folly of not waiting until you have sufficient evidence can be seen in an incident that happened to a salesman friend of mine. A client came to see him during hunting season, sporting his hunting camouflage.

"Did you kill anything today?" my friend asked.

"No, but I took a few 'sound shots.'"

"Sound shots?"

"Yeah, you know. You're up in a tree stand, and you hear something rumbling about in the bushes beneath you. You don't know what it is because you can't see it, but you fire a shot, hoping it will be a deer."

Like pulling the pin of a hand grenade and throwing it across the field before you know whether your target is friend or foe, jumping to premature negative conclusions about others can also have disastrous consequences.

Judging based on suspicion

Baseless suspicion can be a very dangerous thing—especially when it becomes the foundation of a judgment. Consider what it did to King Saul.

It happened as they were coming, when David returned from killing the Philistine, that the women came out of all the cities of Israel, singing and dancing, to meet King Saul, with tambourines, with joy and with musical instruments. The women sang as they played, and said, "Saul has slain his thousands, and David his ten thousands." Then Saul became very angry, for this saying displeased him; and he said, "They have ascribed to David ten thousands, but to me they have ascribed thousands. Now what more can he have but the kingdom?" *Saul looked at David with suspicion from that day on.* (1 Sam. 18:6–9)

Charles Haddon Spurgeon had this to say about the danger of suspicious minds: "Suspicion makes a man a torment to himself and a spy towards others. Once [you] begin to suspect . . . [the] causes for distrust will multiply around you, and your very suspiciousness will create the major part of them. Many a friend has been transformed into an enemy by being suspected."[5]

Judging without divinely appointed authority to do so

God doesn't give everyone the ability to fully investigate every matter. Look again at what Solomon said: "It is the glory of God to conceal a matter, But the glory of kings is to search out a matter" (Prov. 25:2).

Richard Baxter answers the question, "When have I a call to judge another?" Notice the first of his four responses.

> *Answer.* If your office and place require it as a magistrate, pastor, parent, master, tutor, etc. 2. If the safety of the church, or of your neighbor, requires it. 3. If the good of the sinner requires it that you may seek his repentance and reformation. 4. If your own preservation or welfare (or any other duty) requires it.[6]

Judging without first dealing with known sinful motives in your own heart that can blind you from making righteous judgments

People who make judgments about others without first getting the log out of their own eyes (Matt. 7:3–5) do so unlawfully. Jonathan Edwards had some insightful thoughts about this matter.

5. Charles Haddon Spurgeon, *Lectures to My Students* (Grand Rapids: Zondervan, 1979), 325–26.
6. Richard Baxter, *Baxter's Practical Works*, vol. 1 (Soli Deo Gloria), 863.

Very often judgment is passed against others in such a manner that shows the individual is well-pleased in passing it. He is so fervent in judging evil, and judges it on such slight evidence, and carries his judgment to such extremes, that he demonstrates his preference is to do it, and that he loves to think the worst of others. Such a well-pleasedness in judging ill of others is also manifested in our being zealously inclined to declare our judgment, and to speak as well as to think evil of others. It may be speaking of them with ridicule, or with an air of contempt, or in bitterness or with a malicious spirit, or with apparent pleasure in their deficiencies or mistakes.[7]

Judging others on outward appearances such as countenances, body language, and dress

As a biblical counselor, I was trained to look for and evaluate "halo data" (nonverbal clues that may indicate a problem in someone's life). But halo data has to be supported by some kind of verbal substantiation on the part of the counselee before a definitive judgment can be made. Think of the rash judgment Eli made concerning Hannah in 1 Samuel 1:12–14.

> Now it came about, as she continued praying before the LORD, that Eli was watching her mouth. As for Hannah, she was speaking in her heart, only her lips were moving, but her voice was not heard. So Eli thought she was drunk. Then Eli said to her, "How long will you make yourself drunk? Put away your wine from you."

Counselors, of course, are not the only ones who are in danger of making rash judgments about appearances. In marriages, in sibling relationships, at work, and in the church, God's people misjudge the halo data they read from others because they don't think to verify their observations by

7. Jonathan Edwards, *Charity and Its Fruits* (Edinburgh, Scotland: The Banner of Truth Trust, 1855), 212–13 (author's paraphrase).

asking their victims for clarification. Richard Baxter gives tremendous guidance on this matter.

> *Question II.* How far may I judge ill of one by outward appearances, as by the countenance, gestures, and other uncertain but suspicious signs?

> *Answer.* There are some data which are not as much probable, as they are suspicious, and which men are very ordinarily mistaken by: such as those who will judge of a man at the first look of his face; and those who will judge a studious, serious person (such as a lawyer, a judge, or a divine) to be morose or proud, because they are not complimentary, but of few words; or because they have not patience to waste precious hours in hearing an . . . ignorant, self-conceited person talk foolishly. Such censures are but the effects of injudiciousness, unrighteousness, and rash haste. There are other indications that make it evident to a wise and charitable person that the man may be proud, or covetous, or a hypocrite. If with these, there are as many signs to make the contrary probable, we must rather incline to the better than the worse. But if not, we may fear the worst of that person, but not conclude it as a certainty; and therefore we may not in public censures proceed upon such uncertainties, nor venture to divulge them; but only use them to help us exercise caution, and pity, and prayer, and attempt to help them improve.[8]

Judging others based on unilateral reports, unsubstantiated testimony, or hearsay

The last time I was called for jury duty, the district attorney told the jury pool that the crime for which the defendant had been indicted was done in the dark, implying that he had no substantiating evidence (other than the testimony

---

8. Richard Baxter, *Baxter's Practical Works*, vol. 1 (Soli Deo Gloria), 861–62 (author's paraphrase).

of the arresting officer). He wanted to know whether this was going to be a problem for any of us. I explained to him, in the presence of the judge, that if there were no other witnesses *or corroborating evidence,* I might have a difficult time returning a guilty verdict (based on my understanding of biblical jurisprudence). After a perky response from the defense attorneys and a lengthy recess, I learned that I was *not* selected as a juror.

The Bible stresses over and over again the rule that "a single witness shall not rise against a man on account of any iniquity or any sin which he has committed; on the evidence of two or three witnesses a matter shall be confirmed" (Deut. 19:15; cf. Num. 35:30; Deut. 17:6; Matt. 18:16; 1 Tim. 5:19). One witness alone (i.e., one person's word against another) is not sufficient. Baxter proves to be helpful here as well.

> *Question III.* How far may I censure upon the report of others?

> *Answer.* According to the degree of the credibility of the persons, *and evidence* of the narrative; not simply in themselves, but as *compared with all that is to be heard on the contrary part*; else you are partial and unjust. (emphasis added)[9]

Judging based on self as the standard

"I'm the standard, and if you are different from me, you are not the Christian you ought to be." This is the mind-set of those who make this form of rash judgment. These people are often ignorant of the warning of James 4:11. They also forget that God has made us to be different from each other (1 Cor. 4:7), and that there is often more than one way to "skin a cat" (sorry about that, all you cat lovers) or "ice a cake" biblically. Moreover, comparing ourselves with others can be a very unwise activity: "When they measure themselves by themselves and compare

9. Ibid., 862.

themselves with themselves, they are without understanding" (2 Cor. 10:12).

A few examples of this kind of rash judgment include making harsh judgments of others who have personalities, temperaments, tastes, or values that are unusual or different from ours (though they be well within biblical parameters for such things); those who are of a dissimilar social or educational status; those from a different race; those who have unusual medical or physical conditions; or those who have had diverse life experiences.

Why Do We Judge Rashly?

What is behind this tendency to make rash judgments? It is often the desire to find fault in others. Our depravity causes us to delight in finding fault with others. Our self-ishness and pride want us to look better than others. Our bitterness tempts us to get even with those who have hurt us. Our desire to minimize and even justify our own guilt for the way we have sinned against others entices us to exaggerate their faults. Our jealousy makes us afraid of being displaced by others, so we find fault with the competition. We covet what others have, and are angry (envious) that they have what we don't, so we criticize them to convince ourselves that we deserve what they have more than they do. We want (too much) to be analytical and discerning.[10] Our legalism and perfectionism establish a higher standard for ourselves in certain areas than the Bible does, so we judge others to be inferior when they don't measure up to our standards. And, yes, sometimes out of malice, we want to hurt others just for the pleasure of it.

What is it that most motivates you to make snap judgments? Place a check in the appropriate boxes on the next page.

10. This can blind us to the biblical boundaries that charity should not cross.

- ☐ Selfishness
- ☐ Pride
- ☐ Bitterness
- ☐ Desire for vengeance
- ☐ Guilt
- ☐ Covetousness
- ☐ Legalism
- ☐ Perfectionism
- ☐ Malice
- ☐ Other _____
- ☐ Other _____

Ten Ways to Avoid Making Rash Judgments

I will rely heavily on the work of Richard Baxter for many of the points that follow. All of the quotations that are not otherwise credited are either directly taken or paraphrased from his work.

1. Be sure you thoroughly understand the difference between sinful judgments and righteous judgments. Review regularly the various forms of rash judgment that we have considered in this booklet (especially the ones to which you are most prone) until they are programmed into your conscience. Keep a weekly journal of the rash and righteous judgments you make over the next few weeks. At the end of this booklet you'll find the "Judgment Evaluation Worksheet" for you to record and analyze your judgments.

2. Remind yourself often of your own faults and shortcomings, and focus your attention on correcting them. "First take the log out of your own eye" (Matt. 7:5), was Jesus' advice to those engaged in inappropriate judging, "and then you will see clearly to take the speck out of your brother's eye."

He that is truly vile in his own eyes is least inclined to vilify others: and he that judges himself with the greatest penitent severity is the least inclined to be censorious to his brother.[11]

3. Consider yourself to be uncalled and unqualified to judge matters about which you have no authority and limited knowledge. If you really understood how ignorant you usually are of all the necessary facts, you would probably not be so definitive in your judgments. If you understood how much evil resides in your own heart, you would not be so quick to condemn others.

Let not pride make you abuse the Holy Ghost by pretending that he has given you more wisdom in a little time, and with little means and diligence, than your betters have by the holy industry of their lives: Don't presume that God will give more to you in a year than to others in twenty.[12]

Remember that judgment (beyond what we are called to do for the performance of some duty, either by our office, or our private charity, or our self-preservation) is God's prerogative, and that the judge is at the door! [13]

4. Make it your practice to believe the best about others unless there is real evidence to the contrary. Many rash judgments about others would be eliminated if Christians understood and took seriously the biblical precept that "[love] believes all things" (1 Cor. 13:7). While there may be a few exceptions to this rule (cf. Prov. 14:15; 26:24–25), love requires us, in the absence of hard evidence to the contrary, to put the best interpretation on the facts. Practically speaking, this means that if there are ten possible explanations for an action you understood me to take, nine of which are bad, and only one of which is good, unless

11. Richard Baxter, *Baxter's Practical Works*, vol. 1 (Soli Deo Gloria), 863–64.
12. Ibid.
13. Ibid.

there is some form of verifiable evidence to the contrary, love requires you to reject the nine and accept the one.[14]

> We see that people *are very reluctant to judge evil about those they love*. We see this in men toward those who are personal friends and in parents toward their children. They are very ready to think well of them, and to think the best of their qualifications, whether natural or moral. They are much more hesitant than others to take up evil reports of them, and slow to believe what is said against them. They are eager to put the most favorable interpretations on their actions. And the reason is because they love them.[15]

> Censoriousness is contrary to the nature and office of Jesus Christ: he came to pardon sin, and cover the infirmities of his servants, and to cast them behind his back, and into the depth of the sea, and to bury them in his grave; and it is the censurer's work to rake them up, and to make them seem more and greater than they are, and to bring them into the open light.[16]

5. Be sure you fully understand the doctrine of total depravity of all men (sinner and saint), as this will moderate the severity of your judgments. The sin of pride causes us to forget how wicked we are. It causes us to focus on the speck in our neighbor's eye while blinding us to the logs in our own eyes.

We are all made of the same stuff, and it isn't pretty! Noah got drunk. Elijah was a man subject to passions. Abraham was a bigamist. David committed murder and adultery. Jonah ran away from God. Job justified himself rather than God. Peter lied

14. Certainly you may have suspicion about the matter, but you may not slam the gavel down in your mind (or with your lips) and pronounce a judgment until you have all the facts. You may even ask me to explain or clarify my behavior, but unless I tell you otherwise, you are obligated to believe the best about me. Should I verify the *one good reason* you chose to believe (though admittedly it was somewhat of a stretch for you, yet for love's sake, you did) over the *nine bad ones*, you may then say to me with a clear conscience, "That's exactly what I thought your reason was."

15. Jonathan Edwards, *Charity and Its Fruits* (Edinburgh, Scotland: The Banner of Truth Trust, 1855), 214 (author's paraphrase).

16. Richard Baxter, *Baxter's Practical Works*, vol. 1 (Soli Deo Gloria), 864.

three times in the process of denying the Lord. Paul said even of his own teaching companions, "For they all seek after their own interests, not those of Christ Jesus" (Phil. 2:21).

6. Learn to look for and value even the smallest manifestations of God's grace and Christ's character in others, for then you will be able to see in others things for which you can be thankful. Those who make rash judgments seem especially prone to overlook the positive in the process of accentuating the negative. If this is something with which you struggle, let me suggest that you make a list of those individuals about whom you have been most uncharitable in your judgments. Then, think through at least a dozen positive things about each one of them. Finally, thank God regularly for those positive elements of their character. At the back of this booklet you'll find the "Character Appreciation Worksheet" to help facilitate this exercise.

7. Deal quickly with those sins that make you more susceptible to rash judgments. There are often attending sins (sins that accompany and lock arms with the predominant sin) that show up in the lives of those who are prone to make rash judgments. Notice how many of the sins listed in the following passage relate to each other, as well as to rash judgments.

> If anyone advocates a different doctrine and does not agree with sound words, those of our Lord Jesus Christ, and with the doctrine conforming to godliness, he is *conceited* and understands nothing; but he has a *morbid interest in controversial questions [or idle speculations]* and *disputes about words*, out of which arise *envy, strife, abusive language, evil suspicions*, and constant friction between men of depraved mind and deprived of the truth, who suppose that godliness is a means of gain. (1 Tim. 6:3–5)

Keep your eyes peeled for these issues in your heart and life, as they will contribute to and exacerbate your tendency to make rash judgments—bitterness, pride, jealousy, inordinate curiosity, and intolerance (lack of forbearance).

8. *Remember that judging others without mercy makes you liable for being judged without mercy.* As a rule, it is better to err on the side of mercy than on the side of judgment. "For judgment is without mercy to the one who has shown no mercy. Mercy triumphs over judgment" (James 2:13 NKJV; cf. Matt. 5:7; Matt. 18:32–35; Rom. 2:3). Are there not many shortcomings in your life for which you daily want God to show you mercy? Then should you not also be willing to show mercy to those whom you are tempted to judge today? If God's mercies to you are "new every morning" (Lam. 3:23), should you not start every morning with a fresh batch of mercy toward others?

9. *Remember that when the full truth comes out, things often appear far better concerning others than we were willing to judge at first.* Jonathan Edwards makes the case from Scripture.

> When the children of Reuben, and of Gad, and the half tribe of Manasseh had built an altar by Jordan, the rest of Israel heard of it, and presently concluded that they had turned away from the Lord, and rashly resolved to go to war against them. But when the truth came to light, it appeared, on the contrary, that they had erected their altar for a good end, even for the worship of God, as may be seen in the twenty-second chapter of Joshua. Eli thought Hannah was drunk when she came up to the temple; but when the truth came to light, he was satisfied that she was full of grief, and was praying and pouring out her soul before God (1 Samuel 1:12–16). David concluded, from what Ziba told him, that Mephibosheth had manifested a rebellious and treasonable spirit against his crown, and so acted on his censorious judgment, greatly to the injury of the latter; but when the truth came to appear, he saw it was quite otherwise. Elijah judged ill of the state of Israel, that none were true worshippers of God but himself; but when God told him the truth, it appeared that there were seven thousand who had not bowed

the knee to Baal. And how commonly are things very much the same now-a-days! How often, on thorough examination, have we found things better of others than we have heard, and than at first we were ready to judge! There are always two sides to every story, and it is generally wise, and safe, and charitable to take the best; and yet there is probably no one way in which persons are so liable to be wrong, as in presuming the worst is true, and in forming and expressing their judgment of others, and of their actions, without waiting till all the truth is known.[17]

10. *Remember also that making rash judgments about others really is a sin, even if the judgment never comes out of your mouth.* What is it that love does? It "believes all things." Not to believe the best about another when it is biblically necessary to do so is to sin in one's heart. Jesus said, "For from within, out of the heart of men, proceed the evil thoughts" (Mark 7:21). Yet as we have seen, making uncharitable judgments of others is all too common.

Few people . . . know the circumstances and reasons for what you do. They will presume to criticize you before they hear what you have to say. Had they done so, they would have absolved you of all charges in their own mind. It is rare to meet, even among professing believers who are sincerely committed [to Christ], those who are fearful and sensitive about sinning in this area of rash, ungrounded judging.[18]

May God grant you great wisdom as you implement the scriptural directives and guiding principles outlined in this booklet. May you, like your Lord and Savior, Jesus Christ, be equipped to judge, not according to appearance (not based merely on what your eyes see or what your ears hear; cf. Isaiah 11:3–4), but with righteous (biblical) judgment every day of your life.

17. Jonathan Edwards, *Charity and Its Fruits* (Edinburgh, Scotland: The Banner of Truth Trust, 1855).

18. Richard Baxter, Baxter's Practical Works, vol. 1 (Soli Deo Gloria), 188 (author's paraphrase)

Judgment Evaluation Worksheet

On the space provided below, record the questionable judgment you made along with a biblical analysis of it.

1. What were the circumstances surrounding my judgment?

_____

_____

_____

_____

_____

_____

_____

_____

_____

2. What was the exact judgment I made?

_____

_____

_____

_____

_____

3. Was it rash or was it righteous according to Scripture?

_____

- ☐ Did I judge something to be a sin that was not explicitly or implicitly identified as such in the Bible?
- ☐ Was my judgment based on insufficient evidence rather than on the facts?
- ☐ Was my judgment based on my own unsubstantiated suspicions?
- ☐ Was my judgment made without divinely appointed authority?
- ☐ Did I make this judgment without first dealing with known sinful motives in my own heart?
- ☐ Was my judgment based on outward appearances such as countenances, body language, and dress?
- ☐ Was my judgment based on unilateral reports, unsubstantiated testimony, or hearsay?
- ☐ Was my judgment based on self as the standard?

Character Appreciation Worksheet

Initials of person about whom I tend to make uncharitable judgments: _____

Positive characteristics he/she possesses for which I can be thankful:

1. _____

2. _____

3. _____

4. _____

5. _____

6. _____

7. _____

8. _____

9. _____

10. _____

11. _____

12. _____

Prayer of thanksgiving to God for these positive qualities:

_____

_____

_____

_____

_____

_____

_____

_____

_____

_____

_____

_____

_____

_____

_____

_____

_____

Judgment Evaluation Worksheet

On the space provided below, record the questionable judgment you made along with a biblical analysis of it.

1. What were the circumstances surrounding my judgment?

_____

_____

_____

_____

_____

_____

_____

_____

_____

2. What was the exact judgment I made?

_____

_____

_____

_____

_____

3. Was it rash or was it righteous according to Scripture?

_____

- ☐ Did I judge something to be a sin that was not explicitly or implicitly identified as such in the Bible?
- ☐ Was my judgment based on insufficient evidence rather than on the facts?
- ☐ Was my judgment based on my own unsubstantiated suspicions?
- ☐ Was my judgment made without divinely appointed authority?
- ☐ Did I make this judgment without first dealing with known sinful motives in my own heart?
- ☐ Was my judgment based on outward appearances such as countenances, body language, and dress?
- ☐ Was my judgment based on unilateral reports, unsubstantiated testimony, or hearsay?
- ☐ Was my judgment based on self as the standard?

Character Appreciation Worksheet

Initials of person about whom I tend to make uncharitable judgments: _____

Positive characteristics he/she possesses for which I can be thankful:

1. _____

2. _____

3. _____

4. _____

5. _____

6. _____

7. _____

8. _____

9. _____

10. _____

11. _____

12. _____

Prayer of thanksgiving to God for these positive qualities:

_____

_____

_____

_____

_____

_____

_____

_____

_____

_____

_____

_____

_____

_____

_____

_____

_____

_____